I MADE IT

A Biographical Sketch of
Mae Ephriam Stewart

Author: Mae Ephriam Stewart
Foreword Written by: Bishop Charles E. Blake, Sr.

Leadership DevelopME, LLC
Publishing Services

DEDICATION

This book is dedicated to my mom, Mable Ephriam, my dad, Robert T. Ephriam, my darling and loving husband, Lucious Stewart, Bishop Charles E. Blake, Mother Barbara McCoo Lewis, and my lovely Ephriam family.

ACKNOWLEDGEMENTS

This book was made possible by so many wonderful family and friends. I would like to acknowledge my sister, Judge Mablean Ephriam, for her time and patience with me during this process.

I would also like to acknowledge my daughter, Diane Kelly, for her assistance in proofreading and typing. Most of all, for her patience with me. I acknowledge the support of my living siblings and brothers, Lee Ola Wade, Richard Ephriam, Frank Ephriam, Marilyn Walker, my church family Church of God in Christ, and my Pacific Christian Center church family of Santa Maria, Calif.

Finally, I would like to acknowledge the assistance of Jacquelyn Winston for her editing, and Dr. Lawanne' Grant for her guidance in publishing this book.

TABLE OF CONTENTS

FOREWORD

Bishop Charles E. Blake Sr.

As a Christian single woman, as a married woman, as a widow; at every stage of her life, MAE EPHRIAM STEWART, is a pattern to be followed and a lesson to be learned.

I, along with a large group of young adults and teenagers, was privileged to know Mae Ephriam Stewart. Her age was very close to ours, but her maturity and spiritual insight was far beyond ours. She sincerely loved the Lord and sought to follow His Word. She was filled with love and compassion for all in our youth organization in Southern California.

She truly was a model and an example that all of us admired and sought to emulate.

I am proud that she has written this book which will bless succeeding generations who read it.

Bishop Charles E. Blake, Sr.
Presiding Bishop Emeritus
Churches of God in Christ International
Pastor, West Angeles Church of God in Christ,
Los Angeles, California

CHAPTER 1:

MEET MAE

Evangelist Missionary Mae Ephraim Stewart is a soft-spoken, godly woman with a power packed, spirit filled deliverance message. The Lord is her Shepherd, and she shall not want. She states, "I want to be filled all the more with his glory and revelation knowledge."

This woman with a message throughout the land before her time is no stranger to God's work. She is a third generation Church of God in Christ Christian. She was saved during her very young age in Hazlehurst, Mississippi at

Mt. Zion COGIC under the leadership of the late Superintendent, William Levi. After relocating to Los Angeles in 1955 with her parents, she became a member of St. Paul COGIC in Watts, California at 113th and Compton Ave. In the mid-60's, she joined Emmanuel Church of God in Christ under the leadership of the renowned and wise Late Bishop Samuel M. Crouch. She became a faithful member, always wanting to be taught the "true" word of God. So her hunger to know more about him grew. God called Mae to the ministry at an early, young adult age. However, fear grasped hold and she did not accept the challenge. It was not until the age of twenty-eight that she went forth to answer the call. When she did, she was on fire. The Lord blessed her to minister in almost every state conducting revivals, conferences, and seminars.

Many lost souls, young and old, surrendered their lives to the Lord as a result and some are reporting the good works of the lord yet today.

Locally, Evangelist Stewart served as Y.P.W.W. President, Y.W.C.C. President, and Sunday school teacher of the youth department for twenty years. In addition, she became the Y.W.C.C. district president and state youth chairlady for seventeen and a half years, working as a mentor and teacher for all ages. Though she has much love for young people, she does not allow them to play with God.

She was blessed to obtain favor of the young people without having to mince words or tiptoe. During speaking engagements and conferences geared for the young, she poured out her love to them and was very concerned about their souls. Oftentimes she could be heard saying, "Young people, God is not through with you." And of course, they would take heed. Her home became their home on Friday nights after youth service. There was no time for the weary and slothful. Evangelist Stewart's jail ministry led her to minster twice a month to young people in juvenile hall and adults in the San Bernardino jail every 4th Sunday. She remembered the poor by ministering on Skid Row the first Monday of every month. As a single missionary, she traveled twice a year to Haiti for five years. As a married woman, she still provides support to the faithful and miraculous work headed by Mother Eleanor Workman. Haiti has captured a certain part of her heart and she longs for the day when she will be able to return to see the babies and mom. Missionary Stewart believes that all missionaries should take a trip to this land at least once.

In 1980, her heart became burdened with the plight of women, especially in the church. She organized a women's fellowship entitled Women with Awareness Ministry. A woman before her time, the ministry went forth for five years and women from diverse cultures, social and economic backgrounds, saved and unsaved, were delivered from many problems, diseases, and afflictions.

Mae's Words of Wisdom:

"Say what you mean and
mean what you say."

~

"The Bible hasn't changed,
read the Word!"

*These are scriptures that helped
me make it through life and I'm
confident will help you make it too.*

Psalm 23:1

The LORD *is* my Shepherd; I shall not want.

~

I Thessalonians 5:18

In everything give thanks; for this is the will of God in Christ Jesus for you.

● ● ●

CHAPTER 2:

MY STRONG FOUNDATION

A testament to single women, Evangelist Missionary Mae Ephraim, waited on the Lord for her "God ordained, chosen" husband. Always a bridesmaid and counselor and never the bride, God answered her prayers in 1985. At the age of 47, Mae was introduced to her future husband and at the age 47 and a half she became the bride. I present this testimony in honor of the most wonderful Savior of all the world, Jesus Christ, and the two greatest parents there has ever been, Robert T. and

Mable B. Ephraim. My parents were blessed with ten children. They were kind, patient, and long suffering. They taught us by precept and example.

My father's mother had six children, five boys and one girl. She mostly raised the kids alone because their dad was gone. It is my observation that most kids raised by a woman, especially men, are very controlling over women. Usually, this is because their mom would punish them for whatever damage and pains (physical and emotional) she had to experience. However, this observation does not describe my grandmother. She taught her boys to be men. That's why my father, who had only a sixth-grade education, was not intimidated by mother's 12th grade education.

My mom, on the other hand, was raised by her grandmother until she was 12 years old.

Her grandmother was so mean to her because she had dark skin. She came to live with her mother when she married a great, loving, and kind man. My mother's stepdad recognized her intelligence and potential, so he sent her to live with her aunt in Memphis, TN. This was one of the best things that happened to her. They were so loving and kind to mom. It was there she was able to complete her high school education. After returning home, she met my father. They married and immediately had three children.

After that, they moved to a town called Hazlehurst, Mississippi, where the other seven kids were born. Initially, they owned and worked a farm that required a lot of work. While dad plowed and planted, mom did all the other work which took a toll on her health. The decision was made. The family would move away from the farm to the city. Mom began to teach at the local school. On the weekends, she worked as a hairdresser and did sewing for extra income. Her dream was to be a nurse. This dream came true when the family moved to Los Angeles, CA in 1955. My Dad became a butcher for one of the most famous markets in Los Angeles. My mom completed nursing school and became one of the best, according to the hospital she worked at.

Mom loved to travel, but Dad did not. After my baby sister was in Jr. high school, mom went twice a year to church conventions, and once a year to visit her elderly mom. Whenever mom was traveling, Dad and I would work together to help the kids with schoolwork.

Both of my parents were clean people who trained their children well. I recall one day my father had come home from work and two of the neighbors said to him, "We hear Mrs. Ephraim is gone again. What will you do with those kids?" He said to them, "They are as much my kids as hers." My father declared, "You see, a man will do what he has to do and not complain like a boy."

Mom and Dad taught the boys to do everything the girls did, and the same rule applied for the girls. When we asked why, Dad told us that he was teaching us how to be responsible for when we got married and had kids. My parents were showing us how to take care of our future families like they took care of us. This was a lesson and example we love, appreciate, and continue to apply until this day. It is a family legacy that we have passed on to our children.

Dad also taught us that if you make a dime, you save eight cents. As a child, I wondered how that was possible, since you couldn't separate a dime. His reply was to just save the whole dime. My dad advised us that credit should be used for a house and maybe for a car. Anything else needed to be "put on lay away." According to mom, one of my brothers and I learned this lesson better than all the other siblings. I learned that having credit was necessary when I tried to buy my first house. I had to open accounts to establish credit, but remembered what daddy said. I paid my bills and didn't overdo it. I am over eighty and still have excellent credit, thanks to my father's lessons.

In 1964, my father had a stroke. He had to leave his work as a butcher, and my mom insisted on leaving her nursing position. At first, we refused to let her. We promised to step up and take care of our father so she could keep working. Ultimately, though, mom stopped working at the hospital and stayed home to give private care to her husband until his passing.

"Love yourself."

~

"I know who I am and Who's I am."

These are scriptures that helped me make it through life and I'm confident will help you make it too.

<u>Philippians 1:6</u>
Being confident of this very thing, that He who has begun a good work in you will complete *it* until the day of Jesus Christ;

~

Ecclesiastes 12:1

Remember now your Creator in the days of your youth, Before the [a]difficult days come, And the years draw near when you say, "I have no pleasure in them."

● ● ●

CHAPTER 3:

A MAJOR LIFE LESSON

I am the second child out of ten. My mom said I was strong like my father and I did not get along with him until I was about 8 years old. When my brother and I went to school, the kids would fight him because he won most of the games that the children played. In the south, if your skin was deemed too dark, the kids with lighter skin would fight you. Even the teachers would punish and discriminate by whipping you. The last time that happened, I went home and gave my brother a stick and said if you allow anyone else to beat you again I will beat you. The very next day my brother won another game and two of his opponents started a fight with him. My brother used that stick to beat them and from that day on, he had no more trouble.

A few days later, I had my own battle to win. A girl called me a dog, but instead of whipping her, I went home crying. My mom asked, "Mae what's wrong with you?"

"A girl called me a dog." I replied.

"You know you aren't a dog." My mom answered back. That did not help me.

When my dad came home, I ran to meet him crying. I jumped up in his arms.

"What's wrong?" He asked.

"A girl called me a dog," I replied.

"Why are you barking?" He asked. I repeated what had happened.

"Why are you barking?" He repeated. Confused and angry, I jumped out of his arms and ran into the house. My mom asked what happened and I repeated my Dad's question. When dad came into the house, I was sent to my room while they talked. He called me back in the kitchen for a sit-down discussion. His advice to me was, "when anyone calls you out of your name, just say to them 'thank you for telling me who you are.'"

This life lesson has stayed in my heart to this day. No one has ever made me feel bad about myself again.

Later, I went to church and told my youth mother what happened. She gave me the scripture (1 Peter 2:9) which states that I am a royal child. This word increased my faith even more. No one has ever made me feel bad or

can belittle me anymore. I accepted the Lord as
my Savior and began to work in the church.

Mae's Words of Wisdom:

"Good things come to those who wait."

~

"Never judge people."

*These are scriptures that helped me
make it through life and I'm confident
will help you make it too.*

Psalm 46:1

God *is* our refuge and strength,
A very present help in trouble.

John 3:16

For God so loved the world that He
gave His only begotten Son, that
whoever believes in Him should not
perish but have everlasting life.

● ● ●

CHAPTER 4:

THE BIG MOVE

I was born in the state of Crystal Springs, MS. We later moved to Hazlehurst when I was 17yrs. old. My mother said when I was three and a half years old, I told her that I was a city girl. She said, "You cannot spell city."

Throughout the years I continued to let her know that I was a city girl with an intention of moving from Hazlehurst. Growing up, my wonderful mom was sickly, and I had to help with the kids. I loved every moment of it, though, because they were trained well. When

I was in the tenth grade, I reminded my mom that I was leaving, whether she was sick or well. My intention became clearer with age so I let it be known that if the family hadn't relocated by the time I graduated from high school, I would leave and go to California. Mom reminded my father that if I left, she was going too. Mom always wanted to leave the south anyway. Two years before I graduated, my father left and came to California. My father never went back to Mississippi, although he would tell my mom he planned on going back. Unfortunately, the year he said he would go back with her is the year he had a stroke.

Two weeks after relocating to Los Angeles, I got a job at a car wash, working in the office calling the customers to let them know they were ready for pick up. After about six months

I felt this was not the job for me. I had a cousin who cleaned houses, so I did that for about three or four weeks. Again, I felt this was not the job for me either. That's when I asked about where the nearest junior college was located.

Within weeks I was enrolled and started classes, so I could get a job to help my mom with the kids. I took classes for accounting, but realized it wasn't for me either. However, I stuck with it, because I felt like time was running out, and I had to work at something to be able to retire.

After a year at college, I got a job at the county hospital as a clerk for low-income families. After two or three years I could not take it anymore because I would take the women's problems home with me.

As I was attempting to determine my practical livelihood, I was being called to ministry and grappling with surrendering to the call of God. He blessed me to travel all over the world and minister in several countries. Haiti was one of the countries I went to twice a year. My boss would say to me when he knew I was going somewhere to minister, "Are you going to be sick?" I would answer no, but the secretary would say, "Yes, you are." She would pull me aside and explain what was going on. God truly blessed me.

God has been good to me.

"Meet me halfway."

~

"Believe people for who they are."

These are scriptures that helped me make it through life and I'm confident will help you make it too.

<u>Romans 12:1</u>

I beseech[a] you therefore, brethren, by the mercies of God, that you present your bodies a living sacrifice, holy, acceptable to God, which is your reasonable service.

~

Proverbs 3:6

In all your ways acknowledge Him,

And He shall direct your paths.

● ● ●

CHAPTER 5:

PROPHECY FULFILLED

Before I move on, let me talk about my fun days. I was a water lover and thought if we didn't go to the beach at least four times a week we had sinned. That happened until my baby sister graduated from high school and left home to go to college in San Francisco. Now, I don't want anyone to think that I didn't continue to do the work of the Lord had assigned for me to do. I continued to do revivals and work for the Lord. Many doors were opened for me and that helped me to trust God even the more.

The life that has been given to me is truly amazing to me and my family.

From an early age, people would come to me for advice regarding their marriages. I would tell them what I felt God wanted me to tell them. Then, I would go home and ask my mother, "Why do people come to me about their problems, when I am not married or even old enough to be married?" She would say, "They see the wisdom God has given you." Throughout my life, my mom often reminded me I could not do things my peers did because God had a greater plan for me. I remember at a young age I was hanging out my clothes and my neighbor said to me over the fence, "I know what you're thinking." And I said, "How?" He replied, "God has a great plan for your life, and you want to be able to do what others do." He continued with his prophesy, saying, "the few friends you have… still, let some go, because what God is going to do in your life, they would hinder you." This confirmed what my mom always told me.

As I listened to and obeyed the Holy Spirit, God opened doors for me that I never thought would happen. He led me to the right bible college in his time, because I tried twice before, and it never worked out. Some of the students would ask, "why are you here?" They felt I was too old to be a student and I should be the teacher. In spite of being a dark-skinned girl from a low-income family, God opened doors for me. Praise God! He loves us as we are. After I graduated from bible school, God continued to open many doors that exceeded my belief.

My first job in the church was a Sunday school secretary. Then, I became a Sunday school teacher for the youth, and finally, an adult teacher for the Women's Department. After that, the Pastor's wife asked me to teach what is called Y.P.W.W., meaning, " young people willing worker" and I did that for years.

Thanks to my loving mother, the girls in my family had to take piano lessons. I learned well and used this gift to play for the children's choir. The church was small, and I served in many ways. I became the janitor and fundraiser. When the windows were broken, I raised money to put them in.

I went into the neighborhood to witness in the homes that would let me in and listen. The church began to grow first with kids and finally the mothers began to come with the kids. We grew from a handful to a large group. I also served as the choir director and played the piano. Unfortunately, after about five years, the pastor got a little jealous. He threw me out of the church, and the people began to leave, including my parents.

The Lord would not let me go so I stayed until the Lord opened the door for me to go. The way for the Pastor to repent was to ask me to go to Africa with him on a mission trip. I knew then it was time for me to go and left after two weeks. Let me tell you, in times of problems, stay calm and do not let anger or anyone talk you into acting up. God has a plan for whatever He allows to happen. God led me to one of the greatest churches. Emmanuel Church, where the great pastor Bishop Samuel Crouch spoke. There, I became a Sunday school teacher, church announcer, and usher. After a little while, I would attend the international convention. There, the Lord opened doors for me to minister in many churches throughout the states and many countries. I ministered most in Haiti, until I was married.

At my church, the Sunday school president asked me to work with him for a while before working with the State youth chairlady. When she retired, I became the leader of the Youth department for over 25 years. However, before I was married, Rev. James and Barbara Lewis would have me do revivals at their church at least twice a year. Then this poor black girl that was not noticed the Rev. J. W. Mayfield asked me to be the state's chairlady for the State youth department. The Lord blessed me in ways I could never have imagined.

The Elder Charles Blake and I became friends, and one day, he asked me to speak in one of our national youth conventions that were held in Florida. Miraculously, many more doors were opened for this poor black girl. Stay faithful to God and he will do what you could never imagine.

Mae's Words of Wisdom:

"Make God the center of your life."

~

"I am the King's child."

These are scriptures that helped me make it through life and I'm confident will help you make it too.

Matthew 1:21

"And she will bring forth a Son, and you shall call His name JESUS, for He will save His people from their sins."

~

Acts 1:8

"But you shall receive power when the Holy Spirit has come upon you; and you shall be [a]witnesses to Me in Jerusalem, and in all Judea and Samaria, and to the end of the earth."

● ● ●

CHAPTER 6:

THE WAIT IS OVER

One Thanksgiving Day after church, I decided to visit a girlfriend in the hospital. On the way to the hospital, going and coming, I noticed every car that passed me had couples in them. I prayed to God as I traveled, asking how long and he answered so fast. "Not much longer, hold on." The answer came so quickly, I said to God, "You didn't have to say it so fast." When I arrived home, I told my mom what happened, and she laughed and said, "He told you, didn't He?" I agreed. But guess what? He sent one so

---

fast that I tried to send him back! So be careful what you ask or say to God. He has a plan, so trust Him.

The man that God sent let nothing stop him. He kept calling and coming down to see me. Finally, I changed my tune in 1984. I had been asked to come to a church in Oxnard, CA, to do a revival. It was about 50 miles from where I lived in Los Angeles. The "Man", Lucious Stewart, love of my life, was there and heard me speak. He went back to his hometown and asked his Pastor if he knew me, wondering if others had even heard me speak before.

"Yes, I've seen her, but never heard her speak." The Pastor told him. Lucious convinced his pastor to have me come and do a service. Three weeks after I left, he got my phone number from another Pastor and called me. But I would not talk to him. He continued to call until my mom said, "Mae, call that man back." Finally, I did and after 3 or 4 months, I said to him, "You can come down." I would not give my address, but asked one of my friends if he could go to her house to meet. We met at her house before going to lunch. It was a very nice lunch.

On the way home, I had to stop at the drug store. As I was getting out of the car, he said, "Can I ask you a question?"

"Yes," I said.

"Would you marry me?"

"No!" I responded.

"Why not?" He asked.

"You are older than me, and you have children." I replied. He assured me that his children didn't run his life, but he urged me to think on it some more. I told him that I didn't have to think, my answer was no. But, he wouldn't give up and I couldn't insult him. I left home to go and speak at a church out of state.

"I don't work," He said, "I can go with you and play piano."

"No," I said.

"Can I at least call you?" He asked.

"No." I said again. But he would anyway, so much so, until my mom called me and said "Mae, call this man."

When I returned to Los Angeles, Lucious called again, and I made plans for him to come meet my Dad and Mom. Before leaving our visit, he made sure to ask my parents a question.

"May I marry your daughter?"

"Can you support my daughter? How will you handle disagreements? If you all ever have a problem and you feel you can't talk about it, don't hit her. Bring her to me and her mother. We can sort it out," My father said. Lucious answered, "I know what the Bible says, 'He who finds a wife finds a good thing.'" (Ephesians 5:22-31) He was right; our marriage was the greatest thing that could have happened.

"Treat others the way you
want to be treated."

~

"Before going to Bible College, make
sure you are rooted in the Word."
(Quote: The late Bishop Samuel Crouch)

*These are scriptures that helped me
make it through life and I'm confident
will help you make it too.*

Psalm 91:1

He who dwells in the secret

place of the Most High

Shall abide under the shadow

of the Almighty.

~

Matthew 11:28

Come to Me, all *you* who labor and are heavy

laden, and I will give you rest.

● ● ●

CHAPTER 7:

FORGIVENESS IS

MUSIC TO THE SOUL

My church was available, but there was no hotel where I could have the reception, as most of them were booked up. Then, I remembered there was the church I used for a luncheon from time to time. I called them, and the lady said, "You called at the right time." They had only one day open on the calendar. So the great day was on. The wedding was scheduled for May 25, 1985.

It was truly a great wedding with my friends and family. After taking pictures, my sister- in-law had a horse-drawn carriage take us to the reception. My husband asked if this was my plan and I said no.

After the wedding we spent two days in Los Angeles, because I had friends who had come out for the wedding, and one of the couples was going home with us for a few days. After they left we were finally alone. At the age of forty-seven and a half, I was a bride.

Around December of that year, I asked him what he wanted for Christmas. He replied, "I don't need anything." But that wasn't the question! I wanted to do something special for my husband. I realized he did not have a piano at home. Lucious loved singing and playing piano. He often played for his church. I went shopping and found a piano and bought it. I told the store what day to deliver it, making sure someone was there to let them in.

On Christmas morning, I had Lucious cover his eyes and led him downstairs. When we got downstairs, I took the mask off, and when he saw the piano, Lord, what he did was something I will never forget. He sat down and played until I made him get up. After that, he would play each morning while I fixed breakfast or after we ate together.

Three years later, he said one morning he wanted a pool table, and I bought that for him. Whenever one of my brothers or nephews came to visit, he would shoot pool with them for a while, and then go back to the piano and singing.

My darling husband played, sung and served at the shelter until he was too ill to do it anymore. The people fell in love with him, and when he was no longer able to come by, they asked about him. It broke their hearts when I told them he was sick and didn't feel like coming anymore.

Now ladies and gentlemen listen to this, we need love and patience here.

Lucious was a beach freak and so was I. We both loved to travel as well. I had been around the world and the U.S. many times. Lucious had only been to three states and Canada. When he said, "I want to go somewhere," I would say, "When?" He'd always say tomorrow. I would pack that night and the next day we would be gone. His favorite place was Las Vegas. We didn't gamble, but Lucious would remind me that wasn't the reason we were going. He would tell me, "We go so we can be alone and not be bothered with anyone."

I did a lot of things with my husband and went a lot of places I did not want to go, so he could have the fun he never had as a child. Lucious never had a life because he was only nine years old when his father left them. He had to care for his Mom and sisters. So, when we married, I encouraged him to do all the things he wanted to do. We went to the rodeo, car shows, and the fair. Although these were not things I necessarily enjoyed, I never complained. I just went so that he could experience these things and have fun.

I did my best to help Lucious forget his early childhood and the pain. For instance, Lucious never celebrated his birthday before we married. So, each year, I would take him out. We would come home from dinner and have dessert and listen to music. He never received Christmas gifts as a child, and rarely as an adult, even after fatherhood. My family made him feel special. My siblings and mother gave him gifts for all the major holidays, like Christmas and his birthday. So did I. Lucious would say, "Mae, you know that I do not need anything." I would say, "We do not do this because you need things, but because I love you and my family does too."

Marriage wasn't perfect, however. There was one small thing that Lucious did that eventually got on my nerves. Lucious would talk about what his father and mother did to him twice a day. Finally, I had enough, and I said to the Lord, Please, tell me what I should say to him to make him listen instead of angering him. You see, his father left his mother and four sisters for Lucious to care for.

When he was only eleven years old and had to try to find work so he could care for them. The father took four brothers, who were older, with him to the state of Louisiana. Lucious continued to support his family until the girls had all left home and got married. Then he found a lovely lady and got married to her and they had six children of their own. You can see there was hurt. It was sad to think about this happening to a kid so young.

God told me to say, "(Baby) you must forgive your dad, mother, brothers, and the men of the church that hurt you."

"Mae, I have forgiven them, otherwise I cannot be saved." He replied.

"Baby," I said, "You forgave them from your head and not your heart."

After about three or four weeks, he said, "Mae you were so right." I acted like I did not know what he was talking about.

Lucious continued, "What you told me. I forgave them from my head and not my heart. Thank you," Lucious never complained about his father and brothers anymore. People, you see what forgiveness does! (Colossians 3:10). He would often say to me and others, "I know God gave you to me." Lucious had been married to his lovely wife for forty-seven years and they had children. This was a new world for me, but with great parents and a great church that taught me the word of almighty God, I was able to adjust well.

There were other times during our marriage that we got angry with each other, or things did not go as we desired (sometimes, even in bed, during sex). But I remembered what my Father said about forgiveness. He said, "If you don't forgive, people will have power over you. Is that what you want?" I would always say no.

"Then, forgive them." He'd reply *(Matthew 6:4-15)*. Forgiveness is important in all matters. Even with sex. I remembered my Father's admonition about forgiveness after a failed sexual attempt. Sometimes, the sexual act was not always fulfilling. Or, shall, I say, my husband did not always make it. My father told me that, "No one makes it all the time, young nor old." Rather than get angry, I would say, "You owe me and I love getting paid." Thankfully, my husband would say, "I love to pay." That was our way of handling misses. Let me tell you, it works. Cast all your cares on Jesus, not man. 1 Peter 5:17.

"Always say what you mean
and mean what you say."

~

"Be the man or woman you
are called to be."

These are scriptures that helped me make it through life and I'm confident will help you make it too.

Isaiah 50:4
"The Lord GOD has given Me
The tongue of the learned,
That I should know how to speak
A word in season to *him who is* weary.
He awakens Me morning by morning,
He awakens My ear
To hear as the learned.

Joshua 1:5
No man shall *be able to* stand before
you all the days of your life; as I was

with Moses, *so* I will be with you. I will
not leave you nor forsake you.

● ● ●

CHAPTER 8:

THEY WILL

REMEMBER YOU

After Lucious and I had been married for a few years, the police called and asked if they could come and talk with him. He said yes. When they got to the house, they said, we have five of your great-grandsons and we want to know if you want them before we send them to another place. Their father and mother were on drugs. Lucious asked me if I would be willing to take them. "Of course!" I said. The police left and

---

returned, bringing our four great-grandsons to us. They were sweet little boys but had not been trained well and had only been to school for four months in a year. We took them in, trained them, and gave them work to do. They never missed school a day after living with us. I'll never forget the day that one of them was sick. The teacher called and said he needed to come home. I went to pick him up and he cried all the way home! I comforted him by letting him know school will soon be out and the other boys will be home also. The next morning, he was feeling better and was able to attend school. Let me tell you, none of them missed another day for the years we had them. I even enrolled my lovely husband in the classes so he could continue his education. He would sometimes do classes with them. They stayed in school until they graduated from high school. Lucious taught them to work, and they did that until they were married. That's why the Bible says, "Train up a child in the way they should go and when they are old, they will not depart from it. " (Ephesians 6:1)

Lucious and I made Santa Maria, CA our home for more than three decades. My husband and I prayed, and the Lord led me to one of the greatest churches in Santa Maria, where I worked until my lovely husband passed. It was called the Pacific Christian Church, and to this day, the Pastor and his wife call me often to see how I am doing. So, young men and women, stay with the Lord no matter what the devil does. God always has a greater plan. Stay with God and pray. The problem may be a job, marriage, or even family. Just give it to God and he will work it out for your good. Read the Bible daily and have prayer time with God (Colossians 3:18-20).

I would witness to both young and older men and women on the street. So many of them accepted the Lord. My husband would say to me, "You better live right." I would say, "Why?"

"Everywhere we go, somebody says 'I remember you and what you taught us.'" Be blessed as you read and do what the Lord says to you.

"Don't let anyone dump trash on you."

~

"I am a royal child of God."

These are scriptures that helped me make it through life and I'm confident will help you make it too.

Psalms 91:14
"Because he has set his love upon Me,
therefore I will deliver him;
I will set him on high, because
he has known My name."

~

<u>Ephesians 1:10</u>

That in the dispensation of the fullness of the times He might gather together in one all things in Christ, both which are in heaven, and which are on earth — in Him.

● ● ●

CHAPTER 9:

REMAIN HUMBLE & FAITHFUL

I was already involved in my local church work in many areas when I was asked to speak at a church in San Luis Obispo. Some ladies who I did not know got my number from someone and asked me to speak for the women. It was there that I met Alex and Sarah Cruz, who fed men and women on the street. We would cook the food at our local church, Pacific Christian Center, and serve the food to them on the street. One day, the Salvation Army saw and told us we could use their kitchen. After that, God opened the door at the Good Samaritan shelter where I worked with them until I moved. The Lord also blessed me to teach a Women's class every Tuesday.

The Pastor called me three times to ask when I was leaving so he could give me a sendoff. I said, "Thank you Pastor, but I don't need that." My darling husband was so hurt.

That same Sunday, after we were home from dinner, my niece called and asked if she could give my number to someone who had been hurt by her pastor. I agreed and listened to the lady's story. When she finished, I asked if I could share my own experience with her, and she agreed. When I told her my experience, she asked about what I did. I responded, "Nothing! I never got upset." She was in awe, because she felt that what had happened to me was worse than what she'd been through. You must remember, whatever the Lord allows in your life, it works for your good.

Three days later, I got a call from a pastor that I didn't know, so I didn't answer. However, some friends I knew in that state called me and asked if they could give their pastor my number. As usual, I agreed. He called and told me he was going to give the church up.

"No, you are not!" I said to him. Once again, this was an example of the Lord allowing something bad to happen to set you up for something greater than you could have ever imagined.

Mae's Words of Wisdom:

"Be the person Mom and
Dad taught you to be."

~

"Laughter is good, like medicine"

These are scriptures that helped me make it through life and I'm confident will help you make it too.

Hebrews 12:14

Pursue peace with all *people,* and holiness, without which no one will see the Lord:

~

Philippians 2:15

That you may become blameless and harmless, children of God without fault in the midst of a crooked and perverse generation, among whom you shine as lights in the world.

CHAPTER 10:

IT WASN'T EASY BUT...
I MADE IT!

The same night, my husband said to me, "Mae if you sing, I will play the piano." He played so long until I couldn't sing anymore. He sat and watched T.V. for a while before going to bed. After about an hour, he called to me.

"Mae, come to bed."

"Why?" I asked.

"You are mine," He said, smiling.

"For how long?" I replied, getting down to pray. As I was praying, he fell out of the bed, begging me to help him up. I tried, but couldn't, so I called his daughter Artis and the paramedics. They were there so fast I hardly had time to get dressed. They worked on him for 45 minutes. He seemed to be doing better, but his daughter and I thought he should still be taken to the hospital for observation.

Once at the hospital, they took him back. After about 30 minutes, the doctor came out and told us he was gone. That was the hardest thing I had faced. I thought when my mother and father passed away that was it, but let me tell you, there is nothing like the loss of a husband.

Thank God I had relationship with God. He was the only way I was able to get through that. When He says He will be your strength, that word is faithful and true.

Mae's Words of Wisdom:

"God blesses those who wait
on and trust him."

~

"I'm through with the mess."

These are scriptures that helped me make it through life and I'm confident will help you make it too.

Luke 17:3

Take heed to yourselves. If your brother sins against you, rebuke him; and if he repents, forgive him.

~

2 Timothy 1:5

When I call to remembrance the genuine faith that is in you, which dwelt first in your grandmother Lois and your mother Eunice, and I am persuaded is in you also.

I MADE IT.

A TESTIMONY

Mae Stewart's impact on my life

I met Mother Mae Stewart in 1985 in Santa Maria, California. My family and I developed such a strong bond and relationship with Mother Stewart, that she became Mother, Godmother and Grandmother to my family. We served in the same church for several years. She has always been a great inspiration to me and my family. She has a never-ending love for everyone, especially young couples. She taught me how to genuinely love my first wife, Octavia, affectionately known as Tay, to me and my children. She would often pull me aside and give me sound wisdom and good advice, not according to man but according to the Word of God. She inspired me and my wife to work together. Thereby, we could accomplish anything that our heart, mind, and soul wanted.

In 1987, Tay and I bought our first home. From that time on with God on our side and Mother Stewart, a sweet, kind, loving, intelligent, and godly woman standing beside us, we knew we could accomplish everything that we desired in our life. She always told us no matter what happens, stay together, and raise your children in the fear and the admonition of God. In 1993 we bought our second home. This was a great milestone in our life. When others doubted us, Mother Stewart never wavered. She encouraged us every step of the way.

During the years 1992 through 1997, my job reassigned me to another location in Irwindale, California. This was approximately 175 miles from my home. I traveled back and forth for more than five and half years. As you can imagine, this was awfully hard on a young family. However, because of Mother Stewart's unconditional love and great support to my wife and children in my absence, our family bond grew stronger than ever. During the latter part of 1997, the Lord allowed me to return to the area of Santa Maria to continue my career. When I look back over my life, I am in awe of how much of a positive impact Mother Stewart has had on me and my family. I must say, she has truly been the greatest inspiration to us than anyone else that I can think of.

In 2003, the Lord blessed us to purchase our third home, again, inspired and encouraged by Mother Stewart. This house was located next-door to Mother Stewart, who by now, had become Mother, God Mother, and Grand

Mother to my family. We found our perfect home, our refuge and happy place in which to dwell, loving God and loving one another as we were told to do by Mother Mae Stewart.

In 2006, the Lord Himself called my wife, Tay, home to be with Him. Mother Mae Stewart stood beside me through all my ups and downs. She supported me and my sons and guided us through the most difficult time of our lives.

In 2007, the Lord allowed me to meet another young lady, Annette, who would later become my wife. Mother Stewart was there with me at the airport when she first came to visit me. Mothers Stewart and Dad - Deacon Stewart welcomed her with open arms. Mother Stewart and Deacon Stewart allowed us to use their home for a wonderful wedding reception. To this day, I feel deeply in my heart that I owe Mother Stewart my life, for it was her love, prayers and unconditional love that kept me above water when I was sinking.

Living in Santa Maria, California, far away from my home state of Oklahoma, I did not have any close relatives. God surely ordered my steps and put the right people in my life. He gave me a mother and a father to guide me, teach me, and love me as their own son. For that, I am profoundly grateful and thankful. If it had not been for the love and guidance of Mother and Deacon Stewart, where would I be. I thank God for the strict teaching that she instilled in me. We love you Mother Mae Stewart!

Pastor Joe & Lady Annette Marzett
God Power House Ministries
Edmond, Oklahoma